About the Author

Born in Germany, Edgar Rothermich studied music and sound engi[neering] prestigious Tonmeister program at the Berlin Institute of Technology (TU) and the University of Arts (UdK) in Berlin where he graduated in 1989 with a Master's Degree. He worked as a composer and music producer in Berlin, and moved to Los Angeles in 1991 where he continued his work on numerous projects in the music and film industry ("The Celestine Prophecy", "Outer Limits", "Babylon 5", "What the Bleep Do We Know", "Fuel", "Big Money Rustlas").

For the past 20 years Edgar has had a successful musical partnership with electronic music pioneer and founding Tangerine Dream member Christopher Franke. Recently in addition to his collaboration with Christopher, Edgar has been working with other artists, as well as on his own projects.

In 2010 he started to release his solo records in the "Why Not …" series with different styles and genres. The current releases are "Why Not Solo Piano", "Why Not Electronica", "Why Not Electronica Again", and "Why Not 90s Electronica". This previously unreleased album was produced in 1991/1992 by Christopher Franke. All albums are available on Amazon and iTunes, including the 2012 release, the re-recording of the Blade Runner Soundtrack.

In addition to composing music, Edgar Rothermich is writing technical manuals with a unique style, focusing on rich graphics and diagrams to explain concepts and functionality of software applications under his popular GEM series (Graphically Enhanced Manuals). His bestselling titles are available as printed books on Amazon, as Multi-Touch eBooks on the iBooks Store and as pdf downloads from his website.

(some manuals are also available in Deutsch, Español, 简体中文)

www.DingDingMusic.com   GEM@DingDingMusic.com

About the Editor

Many thanks to Tressa Janik for editing and proofreading this manual.

Special Thanks

Special thanks to my beautiful wife, Li, for her love, support, and understanding during those long hours of working on the books. And not to forget my son, Winston. Waiting for him during soccer practice or Chinese class always gives me extra time to work on a few chapters.

The manual is based on Logic Pro X v10.2.3

Manual: Print Version 2016-0613

ISBN-13: 978-1534640948

ISBN-10: 1534640940

About the GEM (Graphically Enhanced Manuals)

> ## UNDERSTAND, not just LEARN
>
> What are Graphically Enhanced Manuals? They're a new type of manual with a visual approach that helps you UNDERSTAND a program, not just LEARN it. No need to read through 500 pages of dry text explanations. Rich graphics and diagrams help you to get that "aha" effect and make it easy to comprehend difficult concepts. The Graphically Enhanced Manuals help you master a program much faster with a much deeper understanding of concepts, features, and workflows in a very intuitive way that is easy to understand.

All titles are available in three different formats:

.... pdf downloads from my website www.DingDingMusic.com/Manuals

.... multi-touch iBooks on Apple's iBooks Store

.... printed books on Amazon.com

(some manuals are also available in Deutsch, Español, 简体中文)

For a list of all the available titles and bundles: www.DingDingMusic.com/Manuals

To be notified about new releases and updates, subscribe to subscribe@DingDingMusic.com

About the Formatting

I use a specific color code in my books:

Green colored text indicates keyboard shortcuts or mouse actions. I use the following abbreviations: **sh** (shift key), **ctr** (control key), **opt** (option key), **cmd** (command key). A plus (+) between the keys means that you have to press all those keys at the same time.

sh+opt+K means: Hold the shift and the option key while pressing the K key.

(light green text in parenthesis indicates the name of the Key Command)

Brown colored text indicates Menu Commands with a greater sign (➤) indicating submenus.

Edit ➤ Source Media ➤ All means "Click on the Edit Menu, scroll down to Source Media, and select the submenu All.

Blue arrows indicate what happens if you click on an item or popup menu

Table of Contents

About This Book

Although the Logic Pro X 10.2.3 update doesn't have a high-profile addition like the Alchemy Plugin in previous updates, it is still packed with tons of new features and improvements, besides the usual bug fixes. The Logic team did an outstanding job with adding all those new features and improvements that might seem just like minor tweaks, but they will definitely have a big impact on your workflow, no matter what type of music you are producing with Logic.

➡ *Official Release Notes*

For a comprehensive list of all the new stuff, you can access the official Release Notes directly from inside Logic by selecting the Main Menu *Help ➤ Release Notes*, which opens your web browser displaying the list on Apple's website. https://support.apple.com/en-us/HT203718

➡ *Why this Book?*

So why did I write this book when all the new features and improvements are listed in the official Release Notes?

💀 Graphically Enhanced

The Release Notes only provide a short text-only description of the new features or the changes. In this book, I provide a more in-depth explanation with lots of graphics, screenshots, and diagrams, and sometimes additional in-depth information of the topic to better understand the changes. You will have a "clear picture" of the changes right away and can start using it immediately.

💀 Hidden Features

The Release Notes often forget to list a few features, so whatever additional changes I stumbled over, found online, or what other users discovered on the various Logic forums, I will also list it here.

Free

I make the pdf and iBooks version of this book available for free - not only as a way to boost my Karma, but also to give back to the Logic community who supported me so far by purchasing my other Logic books.

If you are new to my style of writing Graphically Enhanced Manuals and enjoy this book, then don't forget to check out those Logic books on my website http://LogicProGem.com.

The GEM Advantage

If you've never read any of my other books and you aren't familiar with my Graphically Enhanced Manuals (GEM) series, let me explain my approach. As I mentioned at the beginning, my motto is:

"UNDERSTAND, not just LEARN"

Other manuals (original User Guides or third party books) often provide just a quick way to: "press here and then click there, then that will happen ... now click over there and something else will happen". This will go on for the next couple hundred pages and all you'll do is memorize lots of steps without understanding the reason for doing them in the first place. Even more problematic is that you are stuck when you try to perform a procedure and the promised outcome doesn't happen. You will have no understanding why it didn't happen and, most importantly, what to do in order to make it happen.

Don't get me wrong, I'll also explain all the necessary procedures, but beyond that, the understanding of the underlying concept so you'll know the reason why you have to click here or there. Teaching you "why" develops a much deeper understanding of the application that later enables you to react to "unexpected" situations based on your knowledge. In the end, you will master the application.

And how do I provide that understanding? The key element is the visual approach, presenting easy to understand diagrams that describe an underlying concept better than five pages of descriptions.

The Visual Approach

Here is a summary of the advantages of my Graphically Enhanced Manuals that set them apart from other books:

 **Better Learning**

☑ **Graphics, Graphics, Graphics**

Every feature and concept is explained with rich graphics and illustrations that are not found in any other book or User Guide. These are not just a few screenshots with arrows in it. I take the time to create unique diagrams to illustrate the concepts and workflows.

☑ **Knowledge and Understanding**

The purpose of my manuals is to provide the reader with the knowledge and understanding of an app that is much more valuable than just listing and explaining a set of features.

☑ **Comprehensive**

For any given feature, I list every available command so you can decide which one to use in your workflow. Some of the information is not even found in the app's User Guide.

☑ **For Beginners and Advanced Users**

The graphical approach makes my manuals easy to understand for beginners, but still, the wealth of information and details provide plenty of material, even for the most advanced user.

 **Better Value**

☑ **Three formats**

No other manual is available in all three formats: PDF (from my website), interactive multi-touch iBooks (on Apple's iBooks Store), and printed book (on Amazon).

☑ **Interactive iBooks**

No other manual is available in the enhanced iBooks format. I include an extensive glossary, also with additional graphics. Every term throughout the content of the iBook is linked to the glossary term that lets you popup a little window with the explanations without leaving the page you are currently reading. Every term lists all the entries in the book where it is used and links to other related terms.

☑ **Up-to-date**

No other manual stays up to date with the current version of the app. Due to the rapid update cycles of applications nowadays, most books by major publishers are already outdated by the time they are released. I constantly update my books to stay current with the latest version of an app.

☑ **Free Updates** (pdf, iBook only)

No other manual provides free updates, I do. Whenever I update a book, I email a free download link of the pdf file to current customers. iBooks customers will receive an automatic update notification, and 24 hours after a new update, the printed book will be available on Amazon. They are print-on-demand books, which means, whenever you order a book on Amazon, you get the most recent version and not an outdated one that was sitting in a publisher's warehouse.

Self-published

As a self-published author, I can release my books without any restrictions imposed by a publisher. Rich, full-color graphics and interactive books are usually too expensive to produce for such a limited audience. However, I have read mountains of manuals throughout the 35 years of my professional career as a musician, composer, sound engineer, and teacher, and I am developing these Graphically Enhanced Manuals (GEM) based on that experience, the way I think a manual should be written. This is, as you can imagine, very time consuming and requires a lot of dedication.

However, not having a big publisher also means not having a big advertising budget and the connections to get my books in the available channels of libraries, book stores, and schools. Instead, as a self-published author, I rely on reviews, blogs, referrals, and word of mouth to continue this series.

If you like my "Graphically Enhanced Manuals", you can help me promote these books by referring them to others and maybe taking a minute to write a review on Amazon or the iBooks Store.

Thanks, I appreciate it:

 http://amzn.to/1sP8jvl   http://bit.ly/1oJ7ftQ

Disclaimer: As a non-native English speaker, I try my best to write my manuals with proper grammar and spelling. However, not having a major publisher also means that I don't have a big staff of editors and proofreaders at my disposal. So, if something slips through and it really bothers you, email me at <GrammarPolice@DingDingMusic.com> and I will fix it in the next update. Thanks!

LogicProGEM

Please check out my Logic site "**LogicProGEM**". The link "Blog" contains all the free Logic Articles that I have published on the web and continue to publish. These are in-depth tutorials that use the same concept of rich graphics to cover specific topics related to the use of Logic.

http://LogicProGEM.com

Minimum Requirement

Let's start with the "fine print" ❶, a small little detail that has changed with this Logic update. This small little detail can be a big deal breaker for many users, a reason why they might not be able to use the new update in the first place.

To download this new Logic Pro X update v10.2.3 ❷, you have to have at least OSX 10.10 ("Yosemite" ❸) installed on your computer. Any operating system before that, like OS X 10.9 ("Mavericks" ❹) is not compatible.

It is even worse. If you are still running Mavericks (10.9), you can't upgrade to Yosemite (10.10), because that is an "old" system. You have to upgrade to the current version OSX 10.11 ("El Capitan" ❺). So, you better do your homework regarding the compatibility of the apps you are using on your machine before making any OSX upgrade decision.

LPX v10.2.3

Compatibility:
OS X 10.10 or later, 64-bit processor ❶

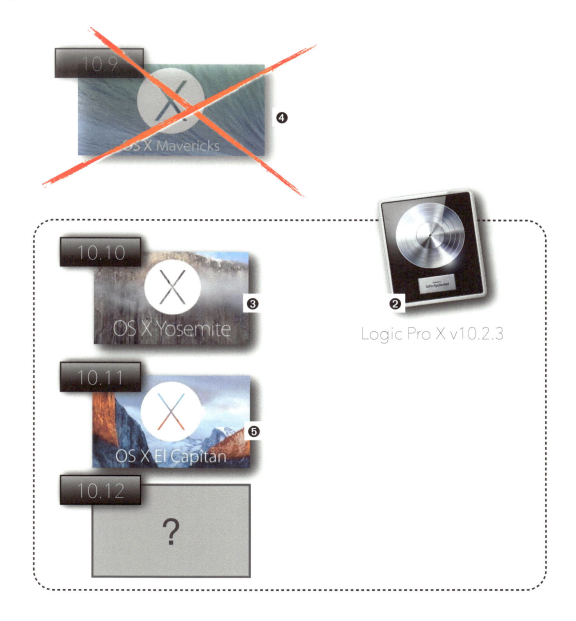

Logic Pro X v10.2.3

Bug Fixes

Everybody has their own "favorite" bug (depending on their workflow) waiting to be fixed. Here is a list of the "fixed" bugs that caused Logic to quit unexpectedly when doing the following actions - not anymore:

- ☑ Overwriting an existing open project from a new project.
- ☑ Option-dragging to copy surround audio files.
- ☑ Multiple audio files with different sample rates than the project are dragged into the tracks area.
- ☑ Sometimes when the computer wakes from sleep.
- ☑ Alchemy opens an EXS instrument containing audio files that are 60 samples or less in size.
- ☑ Importing from a different Alternative of the same project.
- ☑ Sometimes when previewing loops in the Loop Browser.
- ☑ Sometimes when switching between two open projects.
- ☑ After flattening a track stack and then clicking the Score editor tab in the Main window.
- ☑ When resizing the Score Set window.
- ☑ Logic no longer hangs when a note of two bars or longer is recorded from Logic Remote.

The Logic Pro X v10.2.3 update comes with a ton of bug fixes (read through the full Release Notes), but if your "favorite" bug is still not fixed, keep on reporting it to the official feedback page at http://www.apple.com/feedback/logic-pro.html

Improvements

Besides the bug fixes, the update also includes a lot of improvements regarding speed, responsiveness, and even sound quality. Here are just a few from the Release Notes:

- ☑ It now takes less time to load a new instance of Alchemy.
- ☑ The first note played into Alchemy no longer sometimes causes an unexpected CPU spike.
- ☑ Clicking cells in Drum Machine Designer is more responsive, and no longer sometimes causes audio crackles.
- ☑ Logic no longer reinitializes Core Audio if the Plug-in Manager is closed without making any changes.
- ☑ The Channel EQ Analyzer no longer uses CPU when the plug-in window is closed.
- ☑ Projects that include instances of Alchemy are less likely to exhibit unexpected System Overload messages when the Playback + Live Tracks Multithreading preference is enabled.
- ☑ Projects created in Logic Pro 9 or earlier which contain EXS instrument tracks now open faster.
- ☑ Logic no longer sometimes takes an unexpectedly long time to load certain large projects.
- ☑ Logic no longer sometimes performs sluggishly in some projects with the Global Tracks displayed.

More Sounds

Chinese Instruments and Apple Loops

The Logic Pro X 10.2.3 update includes new Apple Loops and Instruments, this time, all Chinese instruments.

Those sounds are not downloaded with the app and you have to install them separately. If you have downloaded the recent GarageBand v10.1.2, then you might have most of those sounds already installed.

- ☑️ Once you open the new Logic 10.2.3, go to the Main Menu *Logic Pro X ➤ Sound Library ➤ Open Sound Library ➤ Open Sound Library Manager...* ❶ to open the Open Sound Library Manager window ❷.

- ☑️ In addition to any sounds that you previously haven't downloaded yet, you will see in the Status columns either "Incomplete" or no entry ❸.

- ☑️ The *World* category ❹ lists the *Percussion* item (that loads the *Chinese Kit*) and the *Stringed* item (that loads the *Pipa* and *Erhu* Instrument). The *Apple Loops* ❺ category lists the new item *Chinese Traditional* with the 300+ new Apple Loops.

- ☑️ Select those checkboxes and *click* the Install button ❻.

- ☑️ The sounds are downloaded in the background and you can see a blue progress bar ❼ under the Display Mode Button on the Control Bar. *Click* on it to open a popover window with the details, plus buttons ❽ to stop or pause/resume the download.

- ☑️ Once the download is completed, an Authorization Dialog pops up, where you enter your OSX Admin Username and Password (not your Apple ID!) ❾.

- ☑️ Once you've entered your credentials, the sounds are installed/placed in your system directory */Library/Application Support/Logic/*. That's why you need the admin authentication.

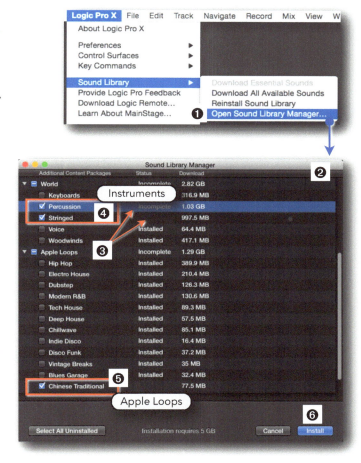

Display Mode Button

Authentication Dialog

➡ **New Instruments**

Erhu   Pipa   Chinese Kit

These are the three new Chinese instruments:

- ☑ **Erhu**: A single-string violin
- ☑ **Pipa**: A guitar-like instrument that sounds like a harp
- ☑ **Chinese Kit**: A collection of Chinese percussion instruments

➡ **Library Browser**

If you open the Library Browser before you have downloaded the new Chinese content, you will see the download arrow ⬇ next to those instruments. Logic will show you any Instruments in the Loop Browser that is available for download but haven't installed yet.

- ▶ **Show Available Downloads**: In the lower-left corner of the Loop Browser, *click* on the Action Button ❶ (gear icon ⚙▾) to open its popup menu and enable *Show Available Downloads* ❷.
  You can also *ctr+click* on any column in the Library Browser to open the Shortcut Menu that has that menu item.
- ▶ **Download Icon** ⬇: Next to any Instrument Category or Instrument in those columns, you will see a download icon ❸ to indicate that there are sounds available for download. In the *World* ➤ *Percussion* category the *Chinese Kit* and in the *World* ➤ *Stringed* category the *Erhu* and *Pipa* Instrument ❹. The actual Instruments are grayed out.
- ▶ *Clicking* on the download icon will start the installation process with the same steps when using the Download Manager.

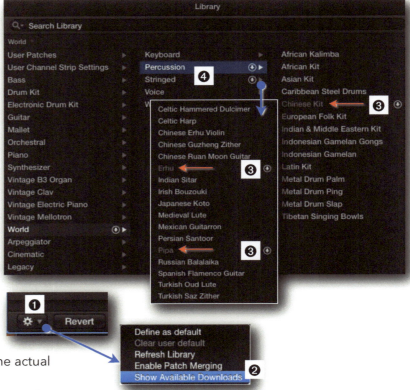

➡ **Loop Browser**

The Loop Browser shows the same download icon ❺ ⬇ for any available Apple Loops that haven't been downloaded yet. Just type Erhu, Pipa, or Chinese in the search field ❻ and you will see all the new Apple Loops.

If you don't have enough space on your boot drive to install all the new content, or like to have them on a separate drive anyway, then please check out my book "Logic Pro X - Tips, Tricks, Secrets #2" where I have detailed instructions on how to "outsource" all those sounds to a separate drive using Symbolic Links.

Quick Swipe Comping

"QuickSwipe/Take Edit" Click Zone Preference

The *Preferences ➤ General ➤ Editing* has a new checkbox called "**Quick Swipe / Take Edit Click Zones**" ❶ that will save you a lot of time clicking around when doing comping.

➡ *Review*

Let's review a few terms and procedures to understand what this checkbox will accomplish:

- ▶ **Click Zone**: A Click Zone is an area on a window that automatically switches the current Cursor Tool to a specific Tool when you move the mouse cursor over it so you don't have to manually switch to that Tool for doing a specific action. For example, the left and right border of a Region is a Click Zone and when moving the mouse cursor over it, it switches to the Trim Tool.

- ▶ **Three Comp Region Buttons**: A Comp Region (also known as Take Folder) has three buttons in the upper-left corner of the Region Header. The *Disclosure Triangle* ❷ (to show/hide the individual Take Lanes), the *Take Folder Menu* ❸ (to open a popup menu), and the *Edit Mode Button* ❹.

- ▶ **Edit Mode Button** ❹: *Clicking* on the Edit Mode Button toggles between two modes:

  - ▪ Take Section Editing (Quick Swipe Comping): In this mode you select the sections on each Take Region to make up the Comp Region.

  - ▪ Take Region Editing: In this mode you can edit the actual Take Regions (move, cut, trim).

➡ *New Functionality*

When you enable the checkbox "**Quick Swipe / Take Edit Click Zones**" ❶, the following behavior will be different:

- ▶ **No Edit Mode Button**: The Edit Mode Button on the Comp Region Header disappears ❺.
- ▶ **Take Region with Click Zones**: The Take Regions, the ones on the individual Take Lanes, now have active Click Zones that automatically switches the functionality of the mouse cursor between Take Section Editing and Take Region Editing.

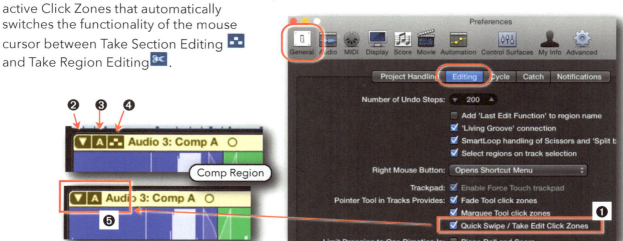

This is how the mouse cursor reacts to Click Zones:

● Upper Half (Take Region Editing ⊞)

The upper half of a Take Region now functions as the Take Region Editing area.

> ▶ Moving the mouse cursor over the upper half will change the cursor to the Pointer Tool ❶ ⬉. Once you *click-hold* on it, it changes to the Hand Tool ❷ ✋ and you can move the Region.

> ▶ Moving the mouse curser over the left or right border of a Take Region will change to the Trim Tool ❸ 🔳 🔳.

● Lower Half (Take Section Editing ✂)

The lower half of a Take Region now functions as the Take Section Editing to do the Quick Swipe comping. It automatically switches between three different Tools depending on where on the lower half of the Take Region you move the mouse cursor over:

> ▶ **Active Take Selection**: *Dragging* an Active Take Selection (the one selected for the Comp Region) will slide that selection. The Cursor Tool changes to the double arrow ◀ ▶ ❹.

> ▶ **Inactive Take Selection**: *Dragging* an inactive Take Selection (gray area) will add that area to the Comp Region. The Cursor Tool changes to the Pipe Tool ❺ ▮.

> ▶ **Selection Border**: *Dragging* the border between an active and inactive selection will move that border left-right. The Cursor Tool changes to the Resize Tool ❻ ✛

● Middle (Marquee Tool)

This optional Click Zone is only active if the "*Marquee Tool click zones*" checkbox ❼ is enabled in *Preferences ➤ General ➤ Editing*. The Cursor Tool changes to the Marquee Tool ❽ ✛ for the standard Marquee Tool functionality.

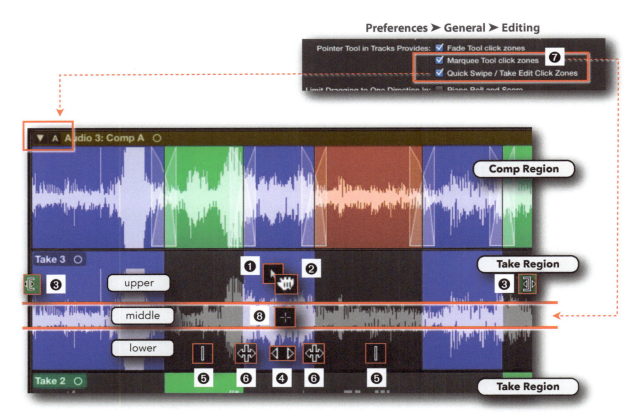

Crossfades in Take Folder are editable

➡ *Review*

The individual Takes on the Comp Region (Take Folder) can be crossfaded. The length (Crossfade Time) and shape (Crossfade Curve) of the crossfades are set in *Preferences ➤ Audio ➤ Editing* ❶. You can change those two settings at any time and all the crossfades of your Comp Region in your entire (!) Project are updated accordingly ❷.

Two things to be aware of:

▶ A Comp Region doesn't get updated visually to show the new crossfade after changing the Preferences. You have to edit (click on) any Take Region for the graphics to get updated visually.

▶ Those Crossfade settings are Preferences, which means, they apply to any Logic Project you open. If you open a Project that used different crossfade settings for its Comp Regions (based on different Preferences at that time), then you Comp Region might sound differently.

➡ *New Functionality*

Now in LPX v10.2.3, you can edit the individual crossfades:

▶ Switch to the Fade Tool ⟩ to edit any of the crossfades on the Comp Region. The functionality is the same as any other crossfade edits between two Regions.

　📌 *Drag* the left or right border ❸ of the white crossfade area ✛ to change the length (Crossfade Time).

　📌 *Drag* inside ❹ the white crossfade area ⟷ to change the shape (Crossfade Curve).

　📌 Please note that you can also Fade-In and Fade-Out the Comp Region ❺.

▶ Any manually edited crossfade will not be updated when you change the Preferences settings

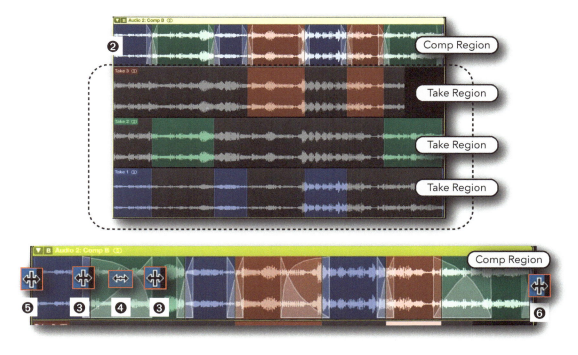

Non-destructive Region Normalize

The Region Inspector for Audio Region has a Gain Parameter ❶ that lets you set a non-destructive gain offset for the selected Audio Region. Now LPX 10.2.3 adds a new command called "**Non-destructive Region Normalize**" ❷ to that functionality.

Here is how it works:

▶ Logic looks at the peak level of the selected Audio Region ❸ and sets the Gain value ❶ so its peak level reaches 0dBFS.

▶ There are two variations of the command that have an affect when you apply the command to multiple selected Regions:

- <u>Individually</u>: Each selected Region is normalized to 0dBFS based on its individual peak level.

- <u>All</u>: Logic looks at the peak level of each selected Region and chooses the one with the highest level (i.e. -9dB) to apply that same Gain value (i.e. +9dB) to all selected Regions.

- The Gain value can even be negative, if the peak level of the Audio Region was above 0dBFS.

- The command is a one time action, so you can change the Gain value to any value at any time.

- The two commands are available in the Local Functions Menu ❹ of the Main Window and they are also available as (unassigned) Key Commands ❺.

Main Window

Toggle Solo Safe on Track Header

Ctr+clicking on a Solo Button of a Channel Strip ❻ toggles **Solo-Safe Mode** for that Channel Strip. Now that click action also works on the Solo Button of the Track Header ❼.

New Project Settings "Clip Length"

➡ *Review*

The Region Inspector has a Parameter called **Clip Length ❶**. When that checkbox is enabled, then any MIDI Note that extends beyond the right border of that MIDI Region ❷ will be turned off at the end of the Clip ❸ (Logic sends a note off command for that note).

➡ *New Functionality*

There is a new tab labeled Clip Length ❹ in the *Project Settings ➤ MIDI ➤ Clip Length*. It has six checkboxes ❺, each one representing a specific MIDI Event Type. When a checkbox is enabled, then Logic sends that MIDI Event with the indicated value (zero, center) at the end of each MIDI Region ❸, if that MIDI Region has the Clip Length checkbox enabled ❶ in its Region Inspector. This guarantees that those MIDI Events are reset to their default values.

💡 **Example:**

In the screenshot below, the MIDI Region has a Modulation (CC#1) value of 59 ❻. At the end of the Region ❸ Logic will send the Event CC#1=0 ❼, because the Clip Length checkbox in the Region Inspector is enabled ❶ and the "Control 1 (Modulation)" checkbox in the Project Settings is also enabled ❺.

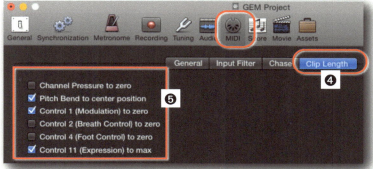

New Display for MIDI Channel No. on the Track Header

If the MIDI Channel Parameter ❶ in the Track Inspector is set to any other MIDI Channel than "*All*", then that number is now displayed in light gray next to the Track Name on that Track Header with the prefix "| Ch" ❷. Before it only displayed a number ❸. Now with the CH prefix it is clear that this number refers to a Channel Number, a MIDI Channel to be specific.

Main Window

Automatic Track Name when importing Audio Files

Logic automatically renames an Audio Track or MIDI Track when you place an Audio Region or MIDI Region (drag from Loop Browser ❹, Project Audio, or Finder) on an empty Track Lane ❺ (with no Regions on it yet):

The conditions, however, have changed:

▶ **10.2.2**: Only Tracks with their default names (Audio 1, Inst 1, etc.) are renamed.

▶ **10.2.3**: Any current Track Name ❻ will be renamed with the name of the file ❼ and even "real" Track Names, the ones that are independent from the Channel Strip Name (I demonstrate in my book "Logic Pro X - Tips, Tricks, Secrets #1" how to create those independent Track Names).

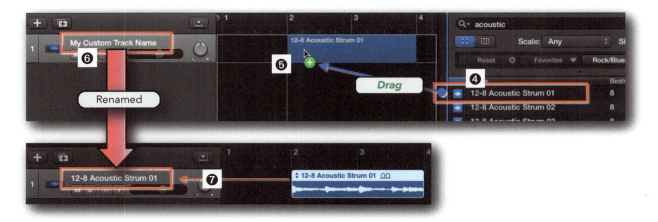

Loop Tool Click Zone on Flexed Audio Region

When Flex View ❶ is enabled (blue button [icon] on the Track Window's Menu Bar) and Flex ❷ is enabled on a Track (blue button [icon] on the Track Header), then its Regions show the various Flex controls ❸. In addition, the Click Zones on a Region are now different.

Remember, a Click Zone is an area on a window that can automatically switch the current Cursor Tool to a different Tool when moving the mouse cursor over it or click on it.

Preferences

Those Click Zones have changed in LPX 10.2.3 depending on the modifier key you press and the status of a checkbox in the *Preferences ➤ General ➤ Editing* called "***Pointer Tool in Tracks Provides Fade Tool click zones***" ❹:

Here are the variations when you use the mouse cursor on the right border of the Region:

▶ ***Click* ❺**: The lower half switches to the Trim Tool and the upper half switches to the Time Compress/Expand Tool. The Fade Tool preference ❹ has no effect.

▶ ***Opt+click***: The upper half switches to the Loop Tool ❻. If the Fade Tool preference is enabled, then there will be three Click Zones ❼. The upper section switches to the Fade Tool, the middle section switches to the Loop Tool, and the lower section has no effect.

▶ ***Sh+opt+click***: The upper half switches to the Loop Tool ❽ regardless of the Fade Tool preference.

Please note that once you drag out a looped section, the right border ❾ of the looped section of a Region has different Click Zones.

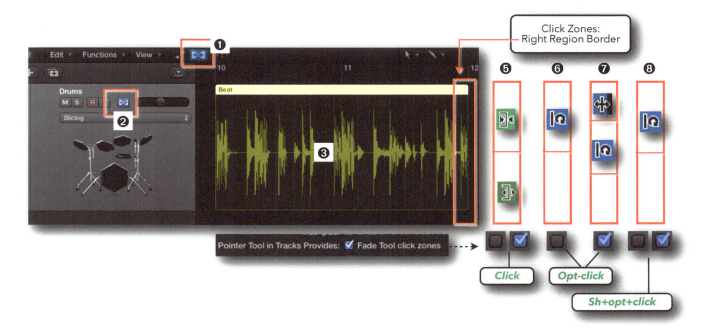

"Splitting Notes" only leaves right note selected

Here is a little improvement that can save you a lot of clicks during MIDI editing:

▶ **10.2.2**: When using the Split command (***cmd+T***) on a selected MIDI Note ❶, you end up with two notes ❷ spliced at the Playhead Position. In 10.2.2, both notes remain selected, so if you use that command to trim the part to the right of the Playhead, you had to deselect the left note first (***sh+click***) before deleting the right note.

▶ **10.2.3**: Now, after splitting a MIDI note, only the right note ❸ remains selected so you can hit the delete key immediately to remove that note. BTW, this is already standard behavior when splitting Regions on the Track Lane.

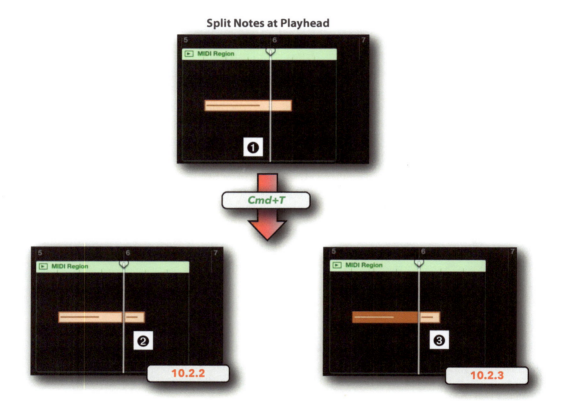

Split Notes at Playhead

3 - New Features in the Main Window

"Zoom to fit Selection" also works in Audio File Editor

Now the various Key Commands for "**Zoom to fit Selection**" also work in the Audio File Editor.

For Example, using the "*Toggle Zoom to fit Selection or All Contents*" ❶ Key Command **Z**, lets you quickly zoom in ❷ and out ❸ of a selection for quick edits by pressing the Z key.

Key Command ❶

Audio File Editor

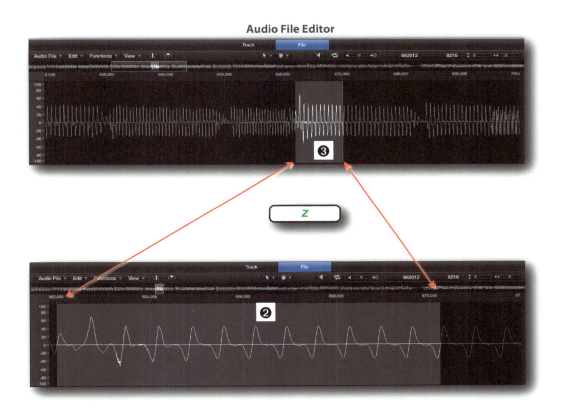

User-definable Key Commands for the Tools Menu

The Logic Pro X update 10.2.1 changed the assigned key equivalent for the Tools Menu ❶ (I call it the Floating Tools Menu) from numbers to more memorable letters (P = Pencil, S = Solo, G = Glue, etc.). Although this can be considered a workflow improvement, some users liked the old numbering system ("change is hard") or would have preferred different key assignments. Now that problem has been solved with the following change in 10.2.3.

(left-click) Tool Menu Button

Attention

The following Tools refer to the left-click Tools that are also listed in the Tool Menu when clicking on the left Tool Menu Button ❷. Please refer to my previous book "Logic Pro X - What's New in 10.2.1" where I discuss the whole (slightly confusing) concept of Tools.

🌑 **Assignable Tools Menu Key Equivalents**

All the Tool are listed in the Key Commands Window ❸ where you can assign your own key equivalents.

Please note that these key equivalents are only active when the Floating Tools Menu is open.

🌑 **Set Previously Set Tool**

"Set Previously Set Tool" ❹ is another new Key Command that lets you toggle between the last selected Tool (left-click Tool) and the current selected Tool.

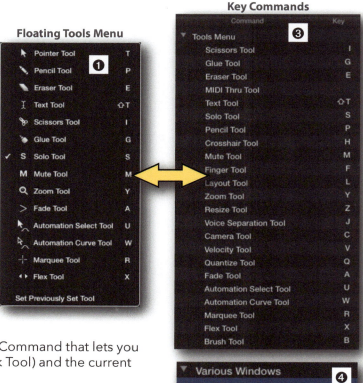

Create Marker at Click Position of Global Tracks

Ctr+clicking on the Global Marker Track ❺ and selecting "Create Marker" from the Shortcut Menu will place the new Marker ❻ at that click position and not at the Playhead as it was in LPX 10.2.2.

Global Marker Track

Quantizing MIDI Events against the Absolute Grid

The following is a big change about how Logic quantizes MIDI Events. Chances are, most users might not even notice it, because they are not aware of the actual procedure (rules) on how MIDI Events where quantized before. (I explain the Quantize procedure in great detail in my book "Logic Pro X - How it Works").

These are the rules:

▶ **10.2.2**: Quantizing MIDI Events will quantize them to the grid of the Region Timeline (Relative Grid) and not the Project Timeline (Absolute Grid). That means, if a MIDI Region doesn't start exactly on a downbeat, the quantized MIDI Events inside the Region will not match-up with the grid of the Project Timeline. In the example below, I have a MIDI Region with three MIDI Events ❶. If I use a 1/1 quantize command ❷, then those Notes are quantized to the 1/1 grid starting at the left border ❸ of the Region. In this case, the third beat of the Project Timeline and not the downbeat ❹ as expected.

▶ **10.2.3**: Now the new behavior is that any command to quantize MIDI Events will quantize them against the Project Timeline ❺ (the Absolute Grid) regardless of the start position of the MIDI Region ❻.

You can use the old method of quantizing against the Region Timeline ❸ (Relative Grid) by holding down the *option* key when selecting a quantize command.

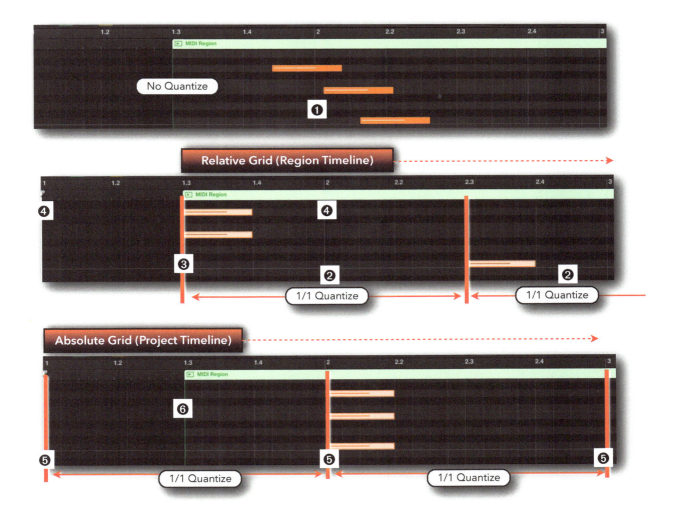

Recording

New "Overlapping Recordings" Labels

The *Project Settings ➤ Recording ➤ Overlapping Recording* ❶ has new menu titles. They've changed from "**No Cycle**" and "**Cycle**" ❷ to "**Cycle off**" and "**Cycle on**" ❸.

A little oversight at the Main Menu Recording, where the submenus still list the old labels ❹.

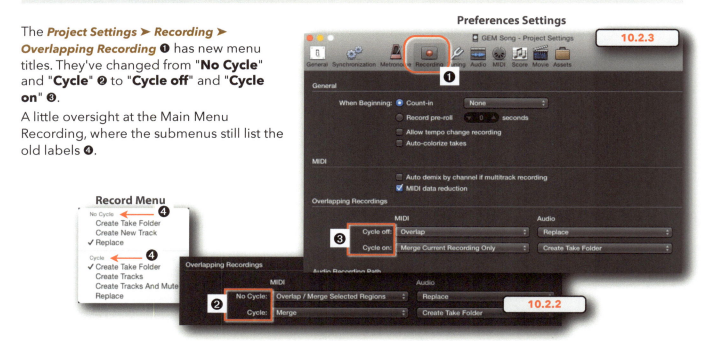

"Replace Button" toggles all Recording Modes to Replace

The Replace Button ❺ 🟧 on the Control Bar (Key Command "*Replace*", number pad **/**) always has priority over the Overlapping Recordings setting!

Now, when you enable the Record Button, all the settings in the Project Settings and the Record Menu switch to Replace ❻ and you cannot change them until you disable the Replace Button. Then all the individual settings are restored the way they were set before.

Be aware of a little graphic bug: The settings are not updated graphically if the *Project Settings ➤ Recordings* window is open. You have to toggle the window to "refresh" it.

Nudge Automation Control Points vertically and horizontally

Finally, Automation Control Points can now be nudged, horizontally and vertically!

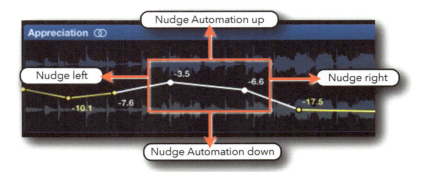

☺ Nudge left-right

Select the Automation Control Points and use the existing Nudge commands to move them left or right on the timeline by the current Nudge Value.

For example:

- 📌 Nudge Buttons ❶ on the Toolbar.
- 📌 Key Commands *Nudge Left* (***opt+ArrowLeft***) and *Nudge Right* (***opt+ArrowRight***) ❷.
- 📌 There is a long list of dedicated Key Commands ❸ for any nudge value that you can now also use for Automation Control Points.

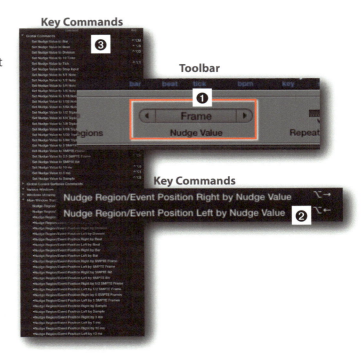

☺ Nudge up-down

LPX 10.2.3 adds four new Key Commands ❹ to nudge the value of selected Automation Control Points 1 step or 10 steps up or down.

- 📌 Nudge Automation up 1 Step
- 📌 Nudge Automation down 1 Step
- 📌 Nudge Automation up 10 Step
- 📌 Nudge Automation down 10 Step

Region Automation for Output Channel Strips

Many Logic users might not even know the existing feature that the following Release Note is referring to:

"When recording Region Based Automation to an Output track, Logic now indicates it is creating a region while recording".

In that context, let me explain the underlying functionality that this improvement is based on.

➡️ *Region Automation*

There are a few things you have to be aware of about Region Automation:

- ▸ **MIDI Regions**: With Region Automation, the Automation Data (Fader Events) is recorded in regular MIDI Regions that you can display and edit in any MIDI Editor (i.e. Event List, MIDI Draw in Piano Roll Editor).

- ▸ **Record Mode**: To record Region Automation, you use the Transport Controls *Record* ❶ 🔴 and not the Automation Modes used for Track Automation.

- ▸ **Audio Tracks**: You cannot record MIDI on an Audio Track, because in Record Mode 🔴, it will record Audio Regions.

- ▸ **Aux Track, Output Track**: You can use Region Automation on Aux Channel Strips and Output Channel Strips ❷. However, first you have to assign a Track ❸ to such a Channel Strip to record the MIDI Region ❹ (containing the Region Automation) on it.

- ▸ **Smart Controls**: You cannot automate any onscreen controls of the Aux or Output Channel Strip (Fader, Pan, etc.) ❺, or Plugin Window, only the onscreen controls that are available in their Smart Controls ❻ window can be recorded as Region Automation.

- ▸ **12.2.3 Improvement**: Although all this functionality already existed in 10.2.2, now when you write Region Automation for Smart Control ❼ of the Output Track, you will see the red MIDI Region ❽ created with the actual Automation Curve displayed on it in real-time.

Creating "New Group" automatically selects the Name Field

Creating a new Channel Strip Group by *clicking* on the Group Slot of a Channel Strip and selecting the last entry in the Group Menu "(new)" ❶ will add that new Group to the Group Inspector ❷.

▶ **LPX 10.2.3** adds a new functionality to that procedure. Once the Group is created, the name field ❸ in the Group Inspector is automatically highlighted (has key focus), so you can start typing a name for that Group right away and hit enter.

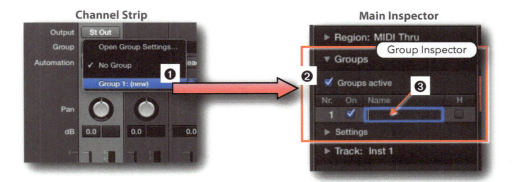

Mute Status is preserved after Solo

When a Channel Strip is muted M and you press the Solo Button S to enable Solo Modo, then it makes sense that the Channel Strip will be un-muted M, so you can listen to the signal on that Channel Strip. However, what happened when you un-soloed S that Channel Strip again didn't make sense in LPX 10.2.2.

▶ **10.2.2**: The Channel Strip remained un-muted, and therefore, left the status of the Channel Strip changed (from Mute M to un-Mute M)

▶ **10.2.3**: Now in LPX 10.2.3, the Channel Strip returns to the Mute status M, the way it was before you soloed the Channel Strip M.

Activity LED for MIDI Channel Strip

The MIDI Channel Strip now has an additional Activity LED ❹ next to the numeric Volume Fader display. The LED lights up when any MIDI Events passed through the Channel Stip.

DMD Window automatically opens when instantiated

If you haven't noticed yet, by being listed in the Plugin Menu ❶, the Drum Machine Designer (DMD) just *pretends* to be a Software Instrument Plugin. Instead, loading that "Plugin" opens a complex Summing Stack with an Ultrabeat Plugin. For an in-depth explanation of the DMD refer to my book "Logic Pro X - How it Works".

The DMD Window ❷ that opens when you click on the Instrument Button (once its loaded) is, therefore, also not a Plugin Window. Instead, it functions as a unique GUI (Graphical User Interface) for that Summing Stack.

With any other Plugin, when you load (insert, instantiate) a Plugin, it will automatically open the Plugin Window by default. That behavior is controlled by the checkbox "Open plug-in window on insertion" ❸ in the *Preferences ➤ Display ➤ Mixer* window (enabled by default).

Maybe because the DMD Window is technically not a Plugin window, it didn't follow that behavior and you had to open it manually after you instantiated the DMD.

> ▶ **LPX 10.2.3**: Now, the DMD Window follows the behavior based on the checkbox ❸ and automatically opens the DMD Window ❷ when instantiated.

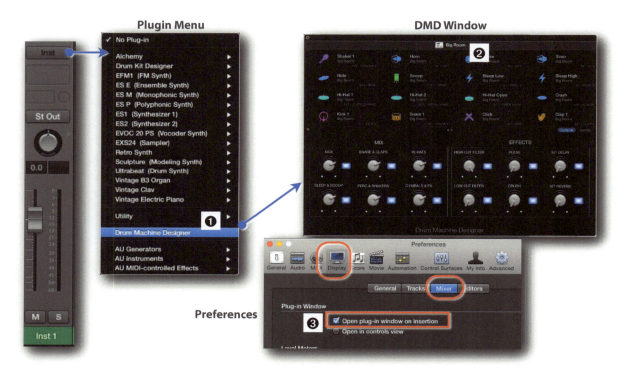

DMD Window stays visible when switching to a different app

The following is another behavior change for the floating DMD Window to act more like a Plugin Window:

> ▶ **10.2.2**: When switching to a different app on your computer, any open DMD Window will disappear, (similar to the behavior of the Key Commands Window) until you switch back to Logic.

> ▶ **10.2.3**: Now when switching to a different app, any open DMD Window will stay visible like any other Plugin Window.

Right-click Cell Icon in DMD opens Icon Window

You can **_right+click_** (or **_ctr+click_**) on any Cell Icon in the DMD Window to open the Icon Window ❶ and select a different icon for that Cell. Be careful, the current icons used on the DMD Window are not part of the Icon Menu. To get the original icon back, you have to load a new sample from the Library Browser that automatically adds the default icon.

💡 No Icon

Selecting the icon "No Icon" ❷ in the *Other* ❸ menu will remove the icon from the Cell ❹ all together. This lets you "clean up" the graphics of the DMD Window and displays only the icons you want on selected Cells.

Warning: Don't **_right+click_** on the main icon on top of the DMD window. Logic will crash if you select an icon from the Icon Window.

DMD Window

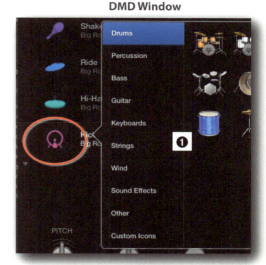

Icon Window

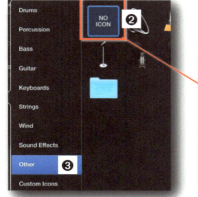

DMD Window

Drag & Drop audio samples directly to Cells

To add a different sample to a Cell in the DMD Window, you open the Library Browser 🖴 on the left side of Logic's Main Window. The Browser automatically switches its displayed content and shows all the audio samples in the Electronic Drums category. **_Click_** on it and it will be loaded in the currently selected Cell.

> ▶ **10.2.3**: Now there is a new drag & drop procedure to add a sample to a Cell:
>
> > ☑️ _**Drag**_ an audio file from the Finder ❺ directly onto the Cell.
> >
> > ☑️ The destination Cell you are dragging over is highlighted in blue ❻.
> >
> > ☑️ The Pointer Tool displays the additional plus sign ➕ (indicating the adding procedures) and the name of the file ❼ you are dragging over.

New Preferences Setting for switching Logic's Localization (Language)

Logic Pro X is available in different languages (localized versions) and automatically switches to the language depending on the language you use for your OSX system.

The *Preferences ➤ Display ➤ General* tab now has a new section *Application* with a Language menu ❶. It lets you switch the language (Localization) for Logic Pro X without changing the language of your OSX system.

The *Default* ❷ item in the menu chooses the current language of your OSX system.

Audio Output Routing for Movies

The *Preferences ➤ Movie* tab has a new checkbox called "**Use Logic Pro X Audio Output**" ❸. The question is, what does that mean?

When importing a video file into your Project, Logic gives you the option to Extract the Audio Track that is embedded in that video file as a separate audio file and puts a new Audio Region, referenced to that audio file, on a new Track in your Project. However, you can still use (play) the original embedded Audio Track from that video file when you playback that video inside Logic. The *Project Settings ➤ Movie* has a slider called Movie Volume ❹, plus a Mute button for that audio signal.

- ▶ **10.2.2**: The Audio Track on the video file is played directly through the default Audio Device that is selected in OSX without going through the Logic Mixer.
- ▶ **10.2.3**: Select the new checkbox ❸ to route the Audio Track on the video file directly through the Audio Device that is selected in Logic (without going through the

Logic Mixer). If not selected, then it is routed to the default Audio Device set for OSX.

Bounce Window: Checkbox "Add to iTunes" is remembered

The settings in the Bounce Window (*cmd+B*) are remembered the next time you open the window. Unfortunately, the "Add to iTunes" checkbox ❶ was not remembered.

But fortunately now in LPX 10.2.3, it remembers the state of that checkbox too.

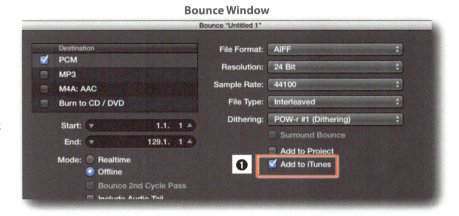

Bounce Window

Flat Folder Icons in All Files Browser Window

Here is a little "improvement" for all Logic users that pay attention to details:
The folder icons in the All Files Browser are updated to conform to the flat design ❷ of OSX 10.10 or later. Finally, that eye sore has been eliminated.

Toggle Force Touch for Trackpad

The *Preferences ➤ Global ➤ Editing* tab has a new checkbox "**Enable Force Touch trackpad**" ❶ that lets you decide if you want to use the Force Touch commands on those newer trackpads.

If you don't have a Force Touch-enabled trackpad connected to your computer, then that option is grayed out.

Here are the available commands:

▶ **Tracks Window**
- Force-click on an empty section of an Audio Track's Track Lane: Opens the Import Audio Dialog Window
- Force-click on an empty section of the MIDI (or Drummer) Track's Track Lane: Creates an empty MIDI (or Drummer) Region
- Force-click on the Ruler: Creates a Marker
- Force-click on a Region: Lets you rename the Region
- Force click on a Track Header: Toggles "Zoom Focused Track"
- Force-click on an empty area of the Track List: Opens "New Tracks Dialog"
- Force click a Region while dragging: Zoom in on the Timeline

▶ **Automation / MIDI Draw**
- Force-click on the background in MIDI Draw: Selects all following Control Points from this position on
- Force-click on a Region with Track Automation enabled: Creates two Control Points at the Region border

▶ **Event List**
- Force-click below Events: Creates a new Event
- Force-click on an Event: Deletes the Event

▶ **Piano Roll**
- Force-click on the background: Creates an Event
- Force-click on an Event: Deletes the Event

▶ **Score Editor**
- Force-click on the background: Creates a Note Event
- Force-click on an Event: Deletes the Event

▶ **Step Editor**
- Force-click on the background: Creates an Event

New Flex Pitch Formant Parameter

If you enable Flex Pitch on a Track, you will see a new Formants Parameter ❷ in the Track Inspector with a popup menu that lets you select the processing regarding unvoiced formants:

▶ **Formants:**
- Process always
- Keep Unvoiced Formants

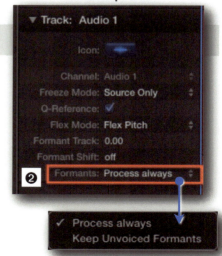

Track Inspector

Score Setting

There is one addition in the *Project Settings* ➤ *Score* ➤ *Chord & Grids* ❶. A new menu item for the Chord Language ❷: **Roman (Do, Re, Mi, Si...)** ❸.

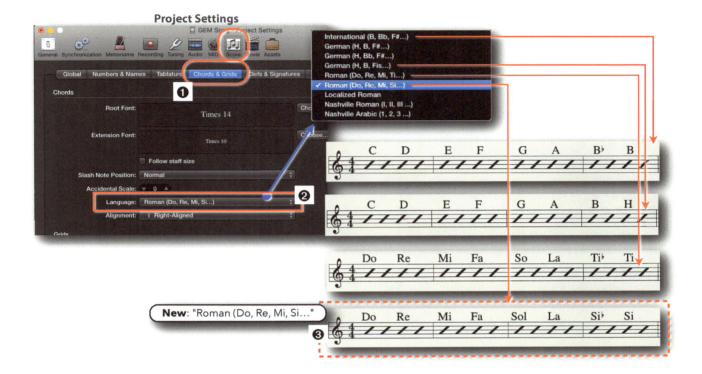

Library Browser Icon opens Plugin Window

The upper section of the Library Browser ❶ (*drag* the divider line ❷ above the search field if not visible) displays the Track Icon ❸ of the currently selected Track ❹. *Double-clicking* on the Icon in the Library Browser will now open the Plugin Window ❺ of the Instrument loaded on the selected Track.

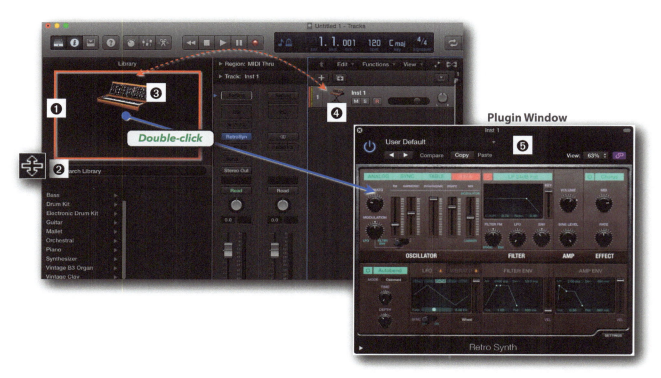

Alchemy

Here is a list of a few improvement in Alchemy:

- ☑ Alchemy now remembers the last used folder location when loading user created IR files.
- ☑ Alchemy now fully supports Unicode/2-byte characters for file names, folder names, patch names, and comments.
- ☑ Emoji symbols now work properly for names and labels in Alchemy.
- ☑ When Alchemy imports a melodic Apple Loop, it now uses the key tag stored in the loop to set the root note.

Alchemy

New "Export Audio to Movie" Default Setting

When you have a movie in your Project and export that movie with your new audio material, you use the command *File ➤ Movie ➤ Export Audio to Movie...* ❶. This command will first open a Save Dialog ❷ where you enter a name and various settings for your new movie file, and then open one more Dialog, *"Choose tracks to export"* ❸.

🌀 **Choose Tracks to Export Dialog**

This window displays all the embedded audio tracks ❹ of the original movie file you are using at that moment in your Project. Here you can configure if you want to include the originally embedded audio track of the original movie file in the new movie file you are about to create in addition to the new audio from your Project.

The checkbox in the second column "Enabled" ❺ was just added in the LPX v10.2.1 update to make it clear if you want to enable (=include) a track or not. Unfortunately, that checkbox was enabled by default and many users that weren't clear about that functionality left it on and were wondering later about the strange results.

▶ **LPX 10.2.3**: Now in this new update, that checkbox is disabled by default. First of all, it doesn't cause any confusion and second, most of the time the embedded audio track is not used when you export your new audio for a movie file.

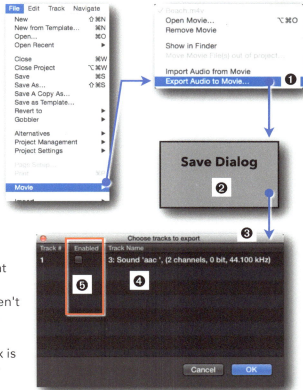

"Snap Edits to Zero Crossing" works again

The option "Snap Edits to Zero Crossing" ❻ in the Snap Menu ❼ works again in 10.2.3. When you trim an Audio Region, the border will snap to the next position of the waveform that crosses the 0dB line on the axis ❽.

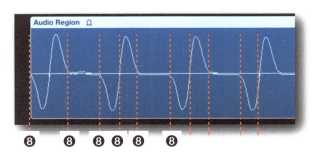

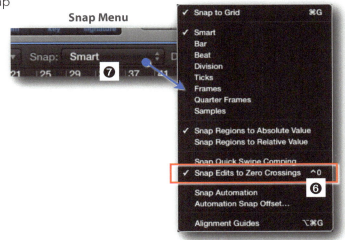

5 - Plugin Makeover

Overview

In addition to the 27 Audio FX Plugins (plus Klopfgeist) that have the new hi-resolution Retina GUI in LPX 10.2.1, the current update 10.2.3 adds 7 more Audio FX Plugins to the "redesign project".

Here are all the Audio FX Plugin submenus, I added shades to indicate which ones have a new GUI or have updated functionality:

- **Red Shade**: These are the Plugins with the new GUI in LPX 10.2.3
- **Red Dot**: These are Plugins with updated functionality in LPX 10.2.3
- **Blue Shade**: These are the Plugins that got the new GUI in LPX 10.2.1
- **Gray Shade**: These are Plugins with an individual GUI that might not get updated
- **Black**: These are Plugins that still have the old blue GUI and might get updated in the future

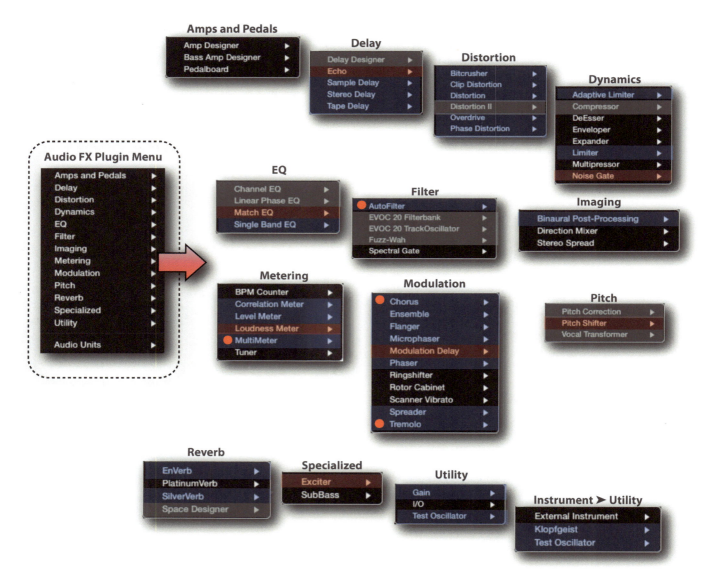

These are the changes in LPX 10.2.3

⚫ **New Plugin**

▶ Meter ➤ **Loudness Meter**

⚫ **Updated Retina GUI**

▶ Delay ➤ **Echo**

▶ Dynamics ➤ **Noise Gate**

▶ EQ ➤ **Match EQ**

▶ Meter ➤ **MultiMeter (surround)**

▶ Modulation ➤ **Modulation Delay**

▶ Pitch ➤ **Pitch Shifter**

▶ Specialized ➤ **Exciter**

⚫ **Updated Functionality**

▶ Filter ➤ **Autofilter**

▶ Meter ➤ **MultiMeter**

▶ Modulation ➤ **Chorus**

▶ Modulation ➤ **Tremolo**

Delay

Echo

The Echo Plugin didn't have a graphic interface before, only the Controls layout with the numeric parameters. Now it has the blue Retina treatment with a few additions:

▶ **Note ❶**: This parameter was named the *Time* ❷ Parameter before. The menu now has two additional values ❸:

- 1/32 dotted
- 1/1 triplet

▶ **Factor ❹**: Similar to other Plugins, you have a button to lower the Note value by half (:2) and a button to double the value (x2).

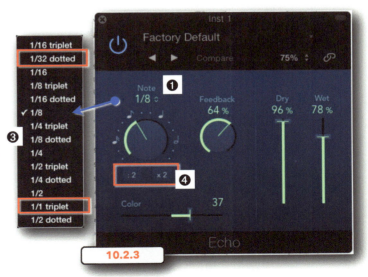

Dynamics

Dynamics

Adaptive Limiter	▶
Compressor	▶
DeEsser	▶
Enveloper	▶
Expander	▶
Limiter	▶
Multipressor	▶
Noise Gate	▶

Noise Gate

The Noise Gate has one major addition, the Ducker.

🔵 Gate

The Gate lets the signal on the Channel Strip go through when the signal is above a specific level (set by the Threshold Parameter) and reduces the signal by a specific dB amount (set by the Reduction Parameter) if it is lower than that Threshold. When choosing the Side Chain function, then the level of an external audio signal determines when the threshold level is met or not.

🔵 Ducker

The Ducker works the other way around and is used, for example, when a DJ talks over music. The Ducker is inserted on the Channel Strip of the music and the DJ signal is used as the Side Chain signal. When the DJ is silent, the music is played at normal level, when the DJ speaks and reaches a specific level (Threshold), then the Ducker reduces the level of the music set by the Ducker Parameter.

▶ **Gate/Ducker**: Switch the functionality between Gate and Ducker by clicking on the corresponding button ❶. The Reduction Parameter ❷ changes to the Ducker Parameter ❸.

▶ **Open/Close LED ❹**: Depending on which LED is on, it shows if the signal on the Channel Strip is *Open* (going through) or *Closed* (reduced). This was a single LED before labeled "Activity"❺.

▶ **Power Button High/Low Cut ❻**: You can enabled/disable the two filters with the Power Button.

▶ **Characteristics ❼**: This new Popup menu lets you choose if the two filters act as Bandpass (only let the frequency band through) or as a Band Reject (let everything through except that frequency band).

10.2.2

10.2.3

Match EQ

The new interface for the Match EQ Plugin is similar to the Channel EQ with nice graphics. There are only minor differences regarding the functionality compared to the old Match EQ Plugin.

▶ **No View Menu ❶**: This popup menu is no longer available.

▶ **Hide Others ❷**: This is an additional checkbox that is available if you select only the left or right channel.

▶ **Action Menu ❸**: The popup menu that you opened before by right-clicking on the Template or Current Button ❹ is now available when *clicking* on the corresponding Action Button ❺ (the gear icon ⚙).

▶ **Channel**: If used in stereo, the Channel popup menu lists the L, R, and L&R options ❻ in the popup menu. If used in surround, you will see the discrete channels ❼ listed.

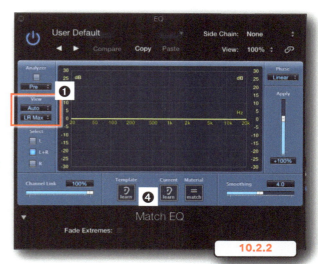

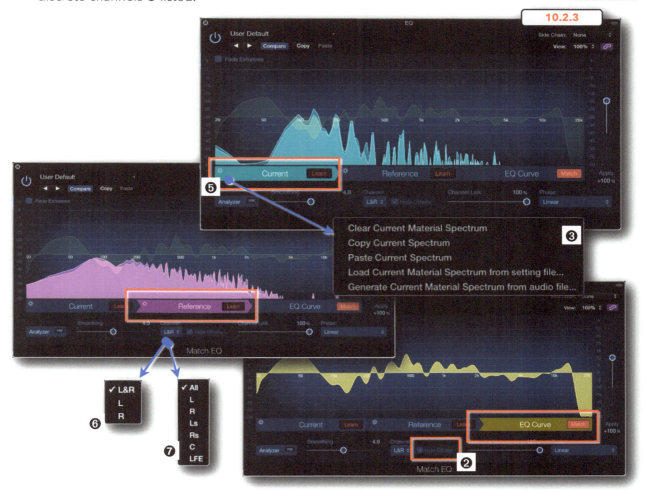

AutoFilter (update)

The AutoFilter already got its GUI makeover in LPX v10.2.1 and now has just two little tweaks:

▶ **Retrigger ❶**: When enabled, the waveform starts at 0° as soon as the Threshold of the Envelope is exceeded. This is actually a parameter that was available in earlier versions of the AutoFilter.

▶ **LFO LED ❷**: The LED that lights up in sync with the LFO rate is a little bit brighter for better visuals.

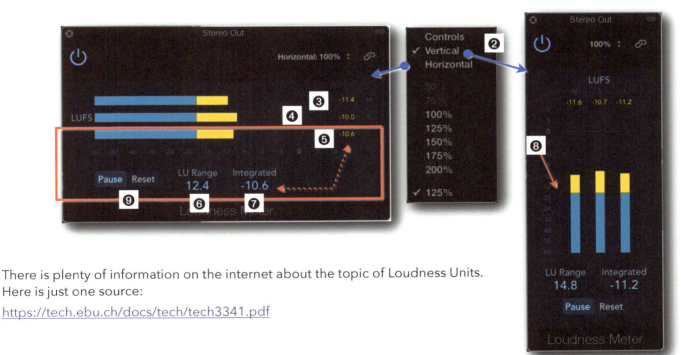

Metering
- BPM Counter ▶
- Correlation Meter ▶
- Level Meter ▶
- Loudness Meter ▶
- ● MultiMeter ▶
- Tuner ▶

Loudness Meter (new)

The makeover of the MultiMeter in LPX v10.2.1 also included a new Loudness Meter ❶. Now, LPX v10.2.3 introduces a complete new Meter Plugin for that functionality, the Loudness Meter. It conveniently lets you measure the Loudness Units (LUFS) without having that big MultiMeter Plugin open, plus it includes some additional functionality.

MultiMeter

▶ **Vertical/Horizontal**: You can change the orientation of the Meter by selecting *Vertical* or *Horizontal* from the View popup menu ❷.

▶ **LUFS-M ❸**: This meter shows the "**M**omentary" level measured with an interval of 400ms.

▶ **LUFS-S ❹**: This meter shows the "**S**hort" level measured with an interval of 3 seconds.

▶ **LUFS-I ❺**: This meter shows the "**I**ntegrated" level measured over time between clicking the "Start" and "Pause" button ❾.

▶ **LU Range ❻**: This numeric value shows the readout for the Loudness Range during measurement.

▶ **Integrated ❼**: This numeric value shows the readout for "Integrated" level during measurement. It is the same level as the LUFS-I meter above.

▶ **Target Level ❽**: You can set a "Target Level" between -30dB and 0dB by dragging the yellow insertion line. That's where the meter starts to change from blue to yellow. Numeric Level readouts next to the meter bar are also displayed in yellow if they fall in that range.

▶ **Start-Pause-Reset Buttons ❾**: These buttons only affect the LUFS-I Meter and the two numeric readouts *LU Range* and *Integrated*. The other two meters are only displayed during playback without any hold functionality.

There is plenty of information on the internet about the topic of Loudness Units. Here is just one source:

https://tech.ebu.ch/docs/tech/tech3341.pdf

MultiMeter (update)

There are a few additions to the MultiMeter:

▶ **View Options ❶**: The View Menu now provides three graphical view options in addition to the Controls View:

- Full **❷**: Displays all the parameters.
- Compact **❸**: Displays only the meters without the parameters in the lower section. ***Ctr+click*** on the display and select from the Shortcut Menu **❹** to switch between Analyzer and Goniometer.
- Meters **❺**: Displays the Level Meter on the right side.

▶ **Separate Peak Hold settings**: The Meters, Analyzer, and Goniometer now have their separate Peak/Hold settings. Please note that you have to click the Hold button (highlighted) to toggle the hold feature. Hold/Reset only affects the LED segments, not the numeric read outs.

- Level **❻**: Peak, Hold, Reset, Return Rate.
- Analyzer **❼**: Peak, Hold, Reset (also click on the display area to reset), Return Rate.
- Goniometer: Peak, Hold, Reset.

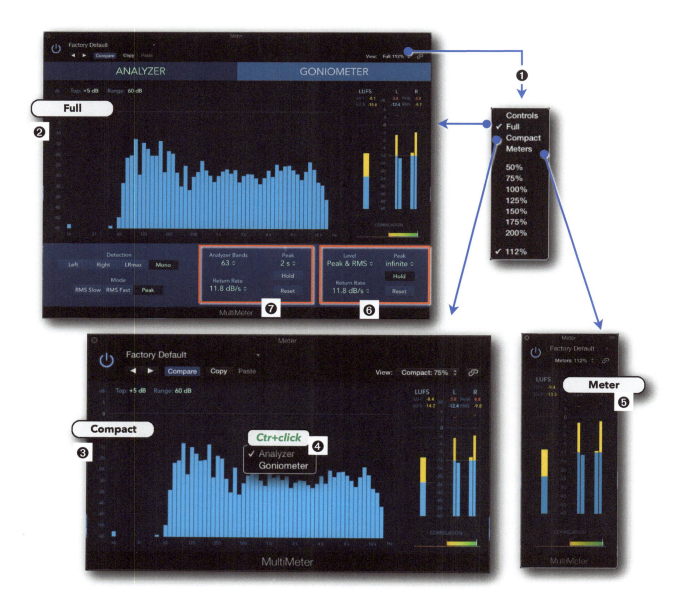

The surround sound version of the MultiMeter is now also updated with the blue retina-enabled GUI.

▶ The Surround MultiMeter has three Display options: Analyzer ❶, Goniometer ❷, and Balance ❸.

▶ The View Menu ❹ also provides these four selections: Controls, Full, Compact, and Meters.

▶ In Compact View, you can *ctr+click* on the display to open a Shortcut Menu ❺ to switch between the three displays.

▶ The only parameter missing from the old Surround Meter is the "Sum" ❻ Detection in the Goniometer.

▶ The Peak/Hold and Level Parameter are the same as in the Stereo Multimeter.

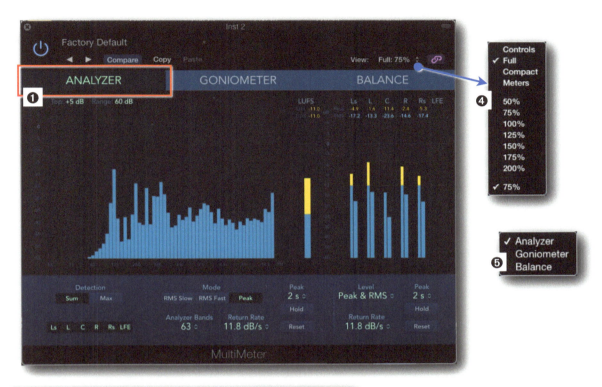

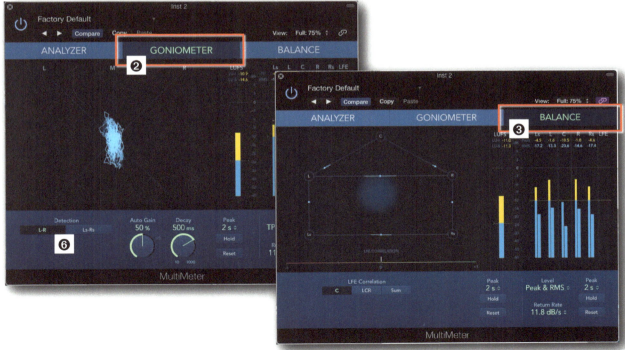

Modulation

Chorus ●
Ensemble ▶
Flanger ▶
Microphaser ▶
Modulation Delay ▶
Phaser ▶
Ringshifter ▶
Rotor Cabinet ▶
Scanner Vibrato ▶
Spreader ▶
Tremolo ●

Chorus (update)

The Chorus Plugin now has on additional button **D-Mode ❶** (now also available in the *Modulation Delay* Plugin).

This is a chorus effect based on the famous "Roland Dimension D". It is a unique sound enhancer for adding spatial and stereo widening effects, where the modulated (pitch shifted) signal is mixed into the adjacent channel, kind of a cross mixing. The effect is similar to adding an additional oscillator to a synth.

If D-Mode is ON, the Mix Knob will be disabled.

Tremolo (update)

The Tremolo Plugin also has one additional control, the **LFO Sync ❷** Button. Its functionality is linked to the Rate Knob:

▶ **Notes ❸**: Turning the Rate Knob left of its center position will display note values (1/64t … 32bars). The LFO Rate is now synced to the Project Tempo and the LFO Sync Button is enabled.

▶ **Hertz ❹**: Turning the Rate Knob right of its center position will display Hz values (0.02Hz … 20Hz). The LFO Rate is not synced to the Project Tempo and the LFO Sync Button is disabled.

▶ **DC ❺**: The Center position displays DC (direct current), no frequency modulation.

▶ **LFO Sync Button ❷**: Switching the LFO Sync button manually will turn the Rate Knob to the left or right side to set it to the corresponding rate.

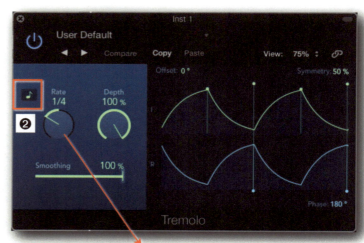

Modulation Delay

The new Modulation Delay Plugin has a two changes:

▶ **D-Mode Button ❶**: This effect is based on the famous "Roland Dimension D", a unique sound enhancer for adding spatial and stereo widening effects, where the modulated (pitch shifted) signal is mixed into the adjacent channel (cross mixing). The effect is similar to adding an additional oscillator to a synth.

> The Output Mix Fader ❺ will be disabled when D-Mode is on.

▶ **Filter**: The filter section is a little bit different than before. Instead of an All Pass Filter ❷ for the left and right channel, you now have a Low Cut and a High Cut Filter ❸, plus a Power Button ❹ to enable the filter.

Pitch Shifter

The Pitch Shifter has the following changes:

▶ **Latency Compensation Button ❶**: This is a new button on the Plugin that lets you toggle Plugin Latency Compensation.

▶ **Timing Menu ❷**: The previous three buttons ❸ for Drums, Speech, and Vocals are now located as menu items in the Timing popup menu ❹ together with the other two options ❺ for Manual and Pitch Tracking.

▶ **Delay, Crossfade ❻**: Those two parameters are only active when Manual is selected in the Timing Menu.

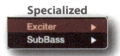

Exciter

There are only two "cosmetic" changes in the Exciter Plugin:

▸ **Dry Signal**: The Input Button ❶ is renamed to "Dry Signal" ❷, which plays only the effect signal if set to "off".

▸ **Frequency**: In addition to changing the Frequency Parameter numerically ❸, you can also drag the dot on top of the vertical line ❹ that represents the frequency value.

6 - Key Command Changes

Changes

I already covered some of the important Key Command additions. Here are all the new ones:

Important Additions

➡ *Floating Tools Menu*

This is the big improvement that lets you assign your own key equivalents to set the left-click Tool from the Floating Tools Menu. Please note that these Key Commands only apply when the Floating Tools Menu is open.

➡ *"Select Previously selected Tool"*

This Key Command toggles the current selected left-click Tool and the previously selected left-click Tool. It works independently for the various Edit windows with their own Tool selection.

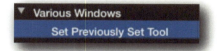

➡ *"Cycle Through Windows (counter-clockwise)"*

There are two "window cycle mechanisms". Pay attention to the exact wording:

- **Windows**: This one cycles through all the open standalone windows.
- **Window Views**: This one cycles through all the visible Window Panes in Logic's Main Window (Tracks Area, Library Browser, Editors, Lists, etc.).

The "Cycle Through Windows" is actually an OSX Shortcut with the name "Move focus to the next window". It also has a counter-clockwise key equivalent *sh+cmd+`* that is not listed in the Key Commands Window.

➡ *Reserved Key Command "Discard Recording"*

The Key Equivalent for the Key Command "Discard Recording and Return to Last Play Position" is now grayed out, which means it is a reserved Key Command that you cannot change.

All new Key Commands

Here are all the Key Commands and the categories they are listed under in the Key Commands Window:

Global

▶ Cycle Through Windows (counter-clockwise)

Various Windows

▶ Set Previously Set Tool

Main Window Tracks and Various Editors

▶ Nudge Automation up 1 Step
▶ Nudge Automation down 1 Step
▶ Nudge Automation up 10 Steps
▶ Nudge Automation down 10 Steps

Main Window Tracks

▶ Non-destructive Region Normalize (All)
▶ Non-destructive Region Normalize (Individually)

Score

▶ Linear Axis View
▶ Wrapped View
▶ Toggle View

Tools Menu

▶ Scissors Tool
▶ Glue Tool
▶ Eraser Tool
▶ MIDI Thru Tool
▶ Text Tool
▶ Solo Tool
▶ Pencil Tool
▶ Crosshair Tool
▶ Mute Tool
▶ Finger Tool
▶ Layout Tool
▶ Zoom Tool
▶ Resize Tool
▶ Voice Separation Tool
▶ Camera Tool
▶ Velocity Tool
▶ Quantize Tool
▶ Fade Tool
▶ Automation Select Tool
▶ Automation Curve Tool
▶ Marquee Tool
▶ Flex Tool
▶ Brush Tool

Conclusion

This concludes my manual " *Logic Pro X - What's New in 10.2.3"*.

If you find my visual approach of explaining features and concepts helpful, please recommend my books to others or maybe write a review on Amazon or the iBooks Store. This will help me to continue this series.
To check out other books in my "Graphically Enhanced Manuals" series, go to my website at:
www.DingDingMusic.com/Manuals

To contact me directly, email me at: GEM@DingDingMusic.com

More information about my day job as a composer and links to my social network sites are on my website:
www.DingDingMusic.com

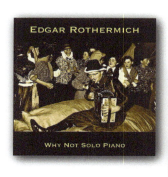
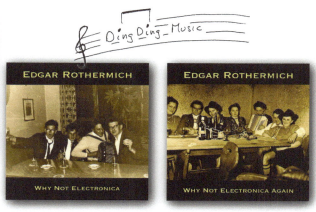
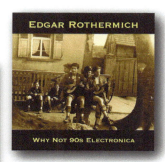

Listen to my music on SoundCloud

Thanks for your interest and your support,

Edgar Rothermich